D0722607

ANIMAL SAFARI

Rhinoceroses

by Kari Schuetz

BELLWETHER MEDIA • MINNEAPOLIS, MN

Note to Librarians, Teachers, and Parents:

Blastoff! Readers are carefully developed by literacy experts and combine standards-based content with developmentally appropriate text.

Level 1 provides the most support through repetition of high-frequency words, light text, predictable sentence patterns, and strong visual support.

Level 2 offers early readers a bit more challenge through varied simple sentences, increased text load, and less repetition of high-frequency words.

Level 3 advances early-fluent readers toward fluency through increased text and concept load, less reliance on visuals, longer sentences, and more literary language.

Level 4 builds reading stamina by providing more text per page, increased use of punctuation, greater variation in sentence patterns, and increasingly challenging vocabulary.

Level 5 encourages children to move from "learning to read" to "reading to learn" by providing even more text, varied writing styles, and less familiar topics.

Whichever book is right for your reader, Blastoff! Readers are the perfect books to build confidence and encourage a love of reading that will last a lifetime!

This edition first published in 2012 by Bellwether Media, Inc.

No part of this publication may be reproduced in whole or in part without written permission of the publisher. For information regarding permission, write to Bellwether Media, Inc., Attention: Permissions Department, 5357 Penn Avenue South, Minneapolis, MN 55419.

Library of Congress Cataloging-in-Publication Data

Schuetz, Kari.
 Rhinoceroses / by Kari Schuetz.
   p. cm. – (Blastoff! readers. Animal safari)
 Includes bibliographical references and index.
 Summary: "Developed by literacy experts for students in kindergarten through grade three, this book introduces rhinoceroses to young readers through leveled text and related photos"–Provided by publisher.
 ISBN 978-1-60014-719-7 (hardcover : alk. paper)
 1. Rhinoceroses–Juvenile literature. I. Title.
 QL737.U63S38 2012
 599.66'8–dc23   2011031239

Printed in the United States of America, North Mankato, MN.

010112   1207

Contents

What Are Rhinoceroses?

Rhinoceroses are one of the largest land **mammals** on Earth. They are also called rhinos.

Rhinos have one
or two horns on
their heads.
The horns are
made of **keratin**.

Where Rhinos Live

Rhinos live in **savannahs**, forests, and **swamps**.

They spend most of the day in the shade. They **graze** on plants and grasses.

Most rhinos live alone. Some rhinos live in groups called **crashes**.

Fighting

Male rhinos fight over females. They use their horns to push and stab.

Sometimes their horns break off. New horns grow to replace them.

Protecting Calves

Female rhinos protect their **calves**. They make loud snorts to scare **predators** away.

Rhinos charge at predators that come too close. Get out of the way!

Glossary

calves—young rhinos

crashes—groups of rhinos that live together

graze—to feed on plants and grasses

keratin—the material from which hair and fingernails are made; rhino horns are made of keratin.

mammals—warm-blooded animals that have backbones and feed their young milk

predators—animals that hunt other animals for food

savannahs—grasslands with few trees

swamps—land areas that are partly covered with water for most of the year

To Learn More

AT THE LIBRARY

Pohl, Kathleen. *Rhinos*. Milwaukee, Wisc.: Weekly Reader Early Learning, 2007.

Swanson, Diane. *A Crash of Rhinos, A Party of Jays: The Wacky Ways We Name Animal Groups*. Toronto, Ont.: Annick Press, 2006.

Terry, Michael. *Rhino's Horns*. London, U.K.: Bloomsburg Publishing, 2002.

ON THE WEB

Learning more about rhinoceroses is as easy as 1, 2, 3.

1. Go to www.factsurfer.com.

2. Enter "rhinoceroses" into the search box.

3. Click the "Surf" button and you will see a list of related Web sites.

With factsurfer.com, finding more information is just a click away.

Index

The images in this book are reproduced through the courtesy of: Jason Prince, front cover, pp. 5, 7; Masterfile, p. 9 (top); PhotoSky 4t com, p. 9 (left); Henry Wilson, p. 9 (right); Anup Shah / npl / Minden Pictures, p. 11; Peter Alvey / Alamy, p. 13; Michael Hutchinson / naturepl.com, p. 15; Anna Yu / Alamy, p. 17; Wildlife Bildagentur GmbH / Kimballstock, p. 19; Bloom Steve / Photolibrary, p. 21.